All-American Fighting Forces

TUSKEGEE AIRMEN

JULIA GARSTECKI

BLACK
RABBIT
BOOKS

Bolt is published by Black Rabbit Books
P.O. Box 3263, Mankato, Minnesota, 56002.
www.blackrabbitbooks.com
Copyright © 2017 Black Rabbit Books

Design and Production by Brad Norr and
Michael Sellner
Photo Research by Rhonda Milbrett

Library of Congress Control Number: 2015954843

HC ISBN: 978-1-68072-004-4   PB ISBN: 978-1-68072-288-8

Printed in the United States at CG Book Printers,
North Mankato, Minnesota, 56003. PO #1794 4/16

Web addresses included in this book were working and appropriate
at the time of publication. The publisher is not responsible for broken
or changed links.

Image Credits
442fw.afrc.af.mil: U.S. Air Force
Photo, 20–21; Alamy: PF-(aircraft), 3,
8–9; AP Images: ASSOCIATED PRESS, 23,
24–25 (background); articles.chicagotribune.com:
32; Corbis: 4–5; Berliner Verlag/Archiv/dpa, 27 (top);
Berliner Verlag, 10–11; Dreamstime: Brian Cogavin, 22;
Artist/Colorist Margaret A. Rogers, MyVintagePhotos.com:
16–17 (airmen); LOC: Frissell, Toni, Back Cover, 1, 28–29
(background); Newscom: akg-images, Cover; Shutterstock:
Bradley L. Grant, 31; Jiripravda, 16–17 (propeller); Tomas
Picka, 6–7; Wikimedia: Office of War Information, 14;
United States Air Force Trademark and Licensing pro-
gram, 27 (wings); USAAF, 19; usaf, 12–13
Every effort has been made to contact copyright
holders for material reproduced in this book.
Any omissions will be rectified in subse-
quent printings if notice is given to
the publisher.

Contents

CHAPTER 1

War above Europe

Two black pilots flew high above **Europe**. Their job was to guard a U.S. **bomber** plane. Suddenly, they spotted an enemy plane. It had to be destroyed.

One pilot steered his **fighter** behind the enemy. But his guns jammed. The enemy tried to escape. But the other pilot fired, taking the enemy's plane down.

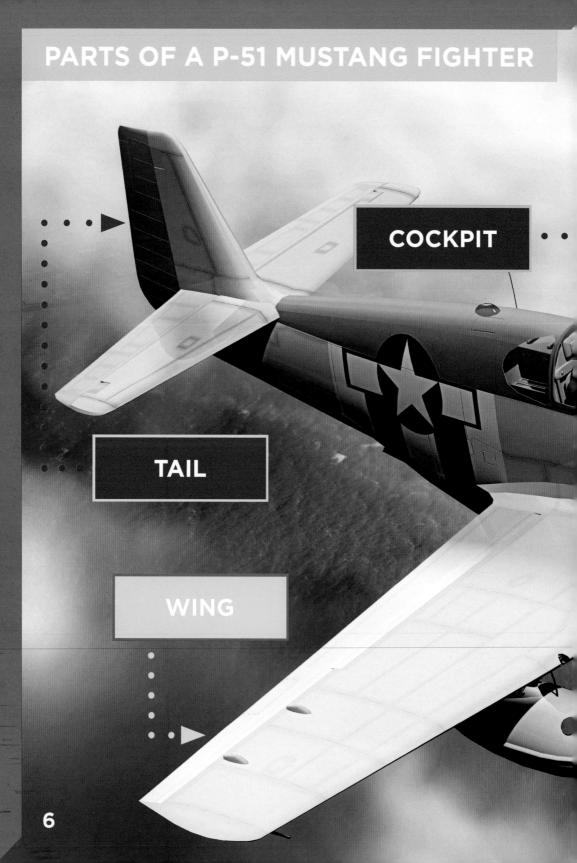

COCKPIT

TAIL

WING

WING

MACHINE GUNS

FUEL TANKS

African American Fighter Pilots

The two pilots were Tuskegee Airmen. The Airmen were the United States' first black pilots. They fought in World War II.

World War II began in 1939. The United States joined the war in 1941. It worked with Great Britain, France, and other countries. They were the **Allies**. They fought against Germany, Japan, and Italy.

ALLIED AND AXIS POWERS

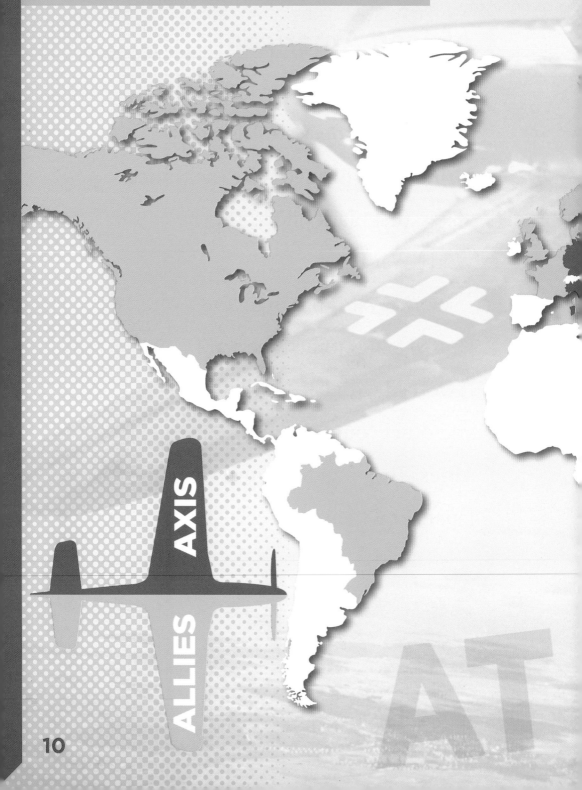

AXIS

ALLIES

AT

CHAPTER 2

Forming the

Tuskegee Airmen

Before the war, African Americans were not allowed to fly military planes. Some leaders felt black people were not smart enough. But others disagreed. In 1941, the army formed a new group. It would train black pilots.

An Army Experiment

The group trained in Tuskegee, Alabama. The men were called Tuskegee Airmen. Some people believed the group would prove black people couldn't fly.

The men did well in training. They proved black men could fly. But some white leaders still did not want black pilots.

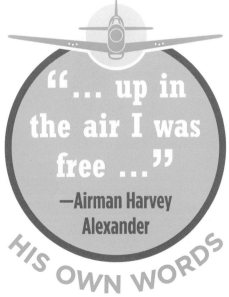

"… up in the air I was free …"
—Airman Harvey Alexander

HIS OWN WORDS

TUSKEGEE
AIRMEN
BY THE NUMBERS

32 HELD AS PRISONERS OF WAR

66 KILLED IN ACTION

ABOUT **445** FOUGHT IN EUROPE

996 TRAINED IN TUSKEGEE

In 1943, the pilots were sent to North Africa. At first, they protected ships at sea.

At last, they received a **mission** to fight. They flew to an enemy island. They destroyed enemy weapons.

Protectors

Then the pilots were given another
job. They flew beside bombers.
They shot at attacking enemy planes.
Finally, leaders saw that black pilots
were as good as white pilots.

Fighting in France

In June 1944, the Allies began an attack in France. Men fought on the ground, at sea, and in the sky. Black and white pilots flew together. Airmen shot German planes. They also attacked enemies on the ground.

One pilot spotted a German ship. He fired. No pilot had ever damaged a ship before!

RED TAILS

Tuskegee pilots painted their planes' tails red. Some called the group "red tails."

FIGHTERS AND BOMBERS

Airmen flew their fighters around bombers.

FLANK ESCORT

REAR ESCORT

SWEEP ESCORT

FLANK ESCORT

CHAPTER 4

An Excellent Record

The Airmen had great flying skills. They also worked well together. It was hard for German pilots to escape them.

The Airmen flew more than 1,500 missions. They destroyed enemy planes and ships. They also proved that skin color didn't affect a person's skills.

Awards Earned by the Tuskegee Airmen

744 Air Medal

96 Distinguished Flying Cross

14 Bronze Star

8 Purple Heart

2 Soldier Medal

1 Silver Star

1 Legion of Merit

TUSKEGEE AIRMEN TIMELINE

APRIL 1939
A law allows the army to train black soldiers.

SEPTEMBER 1939
World War II begins.

MARCH 1941
The army forms a black pilot group.

1940

1941

1942

JULY 1941
The black pilot group meets in Tuskegee, Alabama.

DECEMBER 1941
The United States enters World War II.

JULY 1944
Black pilots shoot down many German planes.

1943

1944

1945

APRIL 1943
The Airmen are sent into battle.

SEPTEMBER 1945
World War II ends.

GLOSSARY

Allies (al-EYZ)—the United States, Great Britain, Soviet Union, France, and other countries that fought against Germany, Italy, and Japan during World War II

Axis (AK-ses)—the countries of Germany, Italy, and Japan during World War II

bomber (BOM-uhr)—an aircraft made to carry and drop bombs

Europe (YUR-up)—the sixth largest continent

fighter (FIGHT-ur)—an aircraft designed to destroy enemy planes and protect bombers

mission (MISH-uhn)—a job assigned to a soldier

BOOKS

Adams, Simon. *World War II.* Eyewitness Books. New York: DK Publishing, 2014.

Gagne, Tammy. *Tuskegee Airmen.* Fact or Fiction? Hockessin, DE: Mitchell Lane Publishers, 2016.

Shea, John M. *The Tuskegee Airmen.* Heroes of Black History. New York: Gareth Stevens Publishing, 2015.

WEBSITES

Focus On: The Tuskegee Airmen
**www.nationalww2museum.org/see-hear/
collections/focus-on/tuskegee-airmen.html**

The Legacy of the Tuskegee Airmen
**www.smithsonianchannel.com/videos/the-legacy-
of-the-tuskegee-airmen/15936**

Tuskegee Airmen-World War II
**www.history.com/topics/world-war-ii/
tuskegee-airmen**

INDEX